Acclaim for
A GRACEFUL FAREWELL

"Sooner or later we all must face the fact that we will pass away. While that may mean that your problems are over, the complications for those left behind are just beginning. For many that means trying to second-guess what you wanted. This book will assist you in making a graceful farewell. It asks all the right questions for you to organize your assets and clearly express your desires so they can be followed after your death. Very thorough in every respect, *A Graceful Farewell* is an excellent workbook… recommended to anyone without reservation."

— *The Midwest Book Review*

"*A Graceful Farewell* is a gentle and easy-to-use guide for adults to put their lives in order. What a gift for your loved ones to know how to implement your critical needs and desires. I will recommend this workbook for my clients and friends."

— Mari Frank, Esq., attorney, author of
Safeguard Your Identity and *From Victim to Victor*

"Though we exercise, diet, and reduce stress, mortality will find us— and most likely unprepared. *A Graceful Farewell* provides simple instructions on how to leave behind an orderly estate. There's even a CD-ROM for those more comfortable with computers than pens. Watson writes in a friendly, clear voice that lessens the fear in taking this important and responsible step."

— Sal Glynn, author of *The Dog Walked Down the Street:
An Outspoken Guide for Writers Who Want to Publish*

Acclaim for
A GRACEFUL FAREWELL

"*A Graceful Farewell* includes so many things that I never thought of — and I'm an organizer! This is the easiest and most user-friendly format I've ever seen. Buy one for every member of your family and for each of your friends. It's one of those gifts that keeps on giving."

— Liz Franklin, author of *How to Get Organized Without Resorting to Arson*

"I can only imagine the hardship my friends and family would face if I became too ill to care for myself, or died, and they had to locate my personal papers and last wishes among my many files, boxes, and hiding places. I've been using an early version of Maggie Watson's workbook and feel a great sense of ease because everything is now accounted for in one place."

— Erica Fielder, Artist, Naturalist

"*A Graceful Farewell* is like the hand of a friend: comforting while at the same time guiding me through the right steps. The workbook format makes the often difficult project of organizing data easy. Most important, this book moved me to begin an earnest contemplation of dying from an accepting and wholesome point of view.
Thank you, Maggie!"

— Gail J. Davis, RDCS, Medical Imaging/Healthcare Provider

A Graceful Farewell

Putting Your Affairs in Order

Maggie Watson

Cypress House

For information, or to order additional copies, please contact:

CYPRESS HOUSE
155 Cypress Street
Fort Bragg, California 95437
800-773-7782
Fax: 707-964-7531
www.cypresshouse.com
Book production by Cypress House

AUTHOR CONTACT:
www.agracefulfarewell.com
e-mail: Maggie@agracefulfarewell.com

PUBLISHER'S CATALOGING-IN PUBLICATION
Watson, M.
  A graceful farewell : putting your affairs in order / Maggie Watson. --
1st ed. -- Fort Bragg, CA : Cypress House, 2006.
  p. ; cm.
  ISBN-13: 978-1879384-68-2
  ISBN-10: 1-879384-68-X
  A workbook formatted to organize personal and financial
  information for your own, and your family's, peace of mind.
  1. Finance, Personal--United States--Handbooks, manuals, etc.
  2. Estate planning--United States--Handbooks, manuals, etc.
  3. Personal information management--United States--Handbooks,
  manuals, etc. 4. Records--Management--Handbooks, manuals,
  etc. I. Title.
  HG179 .W38 2006
  332.024/00973--dc22 0603 2006921025

MANUFACTURED IN THE USA
9 8 7 6 5 4 3
First edition

Acknowledgments

MY HUSBAND, BRUCE ERICKSON, AND MY SON, JULIAN ERICKSON-WATSON, have walked by my side while this book was lived and written.

Special thanks to Pryor Conrad for leaving a gift that launched a book.

I thank the following people for looking over my shoulder, sharing their expertise, and offering their support and love: Norine Newton, Rebecca Deerwater, Wendy Moffatt, Robb Crowder, Jess River, Karen and Richard Green, Jan Austin, Martha Erickson, Margaret Holub, Tom Wodetzki, Jim Tarbell, Joan Katzeff, Norman DeVall, Holly Kuchar, Buffy Maple, Sean Hogan, Michael Shapiro, Millie Milne, David Jones, George Leinen, Michael Coutré, Kathy Warner, J. Redwing Keyssar, Joanna Wigginton, Jerry Minnick, Joshua Slocum, Claire Ellis, Donald and Patricia Watson, Gabriele Fienburgh, Mary Jane Devore, Jimmy and Linda Reynolds, Annette Jarvie, Jennifer Tyler, Linda Jupiter, Bob Lorentzen, Don Abels, Cypress House, and Sally Howell. All were instrumental in getting this book researched, written, and off my desk.

And to those I've omitted, I truly appreciate all the help you gave me over the years as this book evolved.

Safeguard Your Privacy.

This is a personal and private document.
It should be shared only with the executors / trustees / guardians
of your estate and with other designated individuals whom you trust.

Contents

Introduction

THE PROMISE OF THIS WORKBOOK IS THAT IT WILL GIVE YOU PEACE OF MIND. If you take the time to complete this, you'll be confident that your affairs are in order—known and locatable—and that there are clear instructions for those left behind. It will allow your family and friends to deal with the details of your death or incapacity with comparative ease, unhampered at this important time by missing or nonexistent information.

We have all heard stories of families being torn apart because a loved one was not clear about funeral plans, or the daughter who could not claim the life insurance because Mom hid the policy so well that no one could find it. This book can prevent any of these occurrences, and save your loved ones needless additional stress after your death.

The workbook was conceived after working with a friend whose partner had died after a long illness. The partner left a true gift, in the form of a three-ring binder. Inside were categories of information: banking, insurance, investments, and instructions on after-death wishes, etc. I saw that the real importance of the binder lay in there being no confusion about what to do, especially about cremation arrangements. My friend was able to move ahead with the activities needing his attention while at the same time grieving the loss of his partner.

While I was working on the workbook, my friend, Alysoun, was dying. She asked me to be one of her trustees, and though the book was in its early stages, we used it to help set out her wishes before and after death. I needed very clear instructions about everything, even down to where she wanted her clothes to go, and we laughed a lot about all the different categories I wanted to include. When she died, the book was an invaluable resource: it contained all the information for the immediate purpose of carrying out her wishes. Having these instructions enabled me and Alysoun's other beloved friends to do all the necessary activities with confidence. We were not bogged down in uncertainties. We could grieve and still get the work done with humor and love. Carrying out Alysoun's wishes became an honor and a privilege.

With this workbook, you can make this possible for your loved ones.

How to Use this Workbook

THIS BOOK CAN ASSIST YOU IN TWO WAYS:

- by providing a model or outline for how you can set up your filing system;

- by getting your affairs in order, with locatable files and information, complete and up-to-date documents, and clear instructions for your loved ones to follow.

It's a good idea to spend some time looking through the workbook before you begin to fill in the blanks. It will familiarize you with the task at hand and begin to give you an idea of what information you'll need to fill in the various pages. The book is designed so that you can remove those sections that apply to you and put them in a binder.

Once you start, it's fine to take your time—this is an important document. You may need time to reflect on what you need to include. These might be questions you haven't asked yourself before. Whether you complete it alone or with your family and friends, it isn't something that needs to be done in one sitting.

SOME TIPS

♦ For couples, have two of these books—one for each of you. Some information will be duplicated, but keeping it separate is clearer and simpler, and there are areas that need to reflect each person's unique wishes and situation.

♦ Once you complete this workbook, update it annually. Find a time of year that works for you, and stick to it!

♦ If you live in two places, keep a copy of it in each location.

♦ Tell your executor/trustee where to find the book.

♦ Include copies of important papers (will, trusts, etc.) in your completed binder, and list the location(s) of all original documents.

♦ If you complete only one section from this book, fill in the location checklist. Remember: location, location, location!

♦ If you use this workbook in book form and choose not to fill out a page, draw a line through that page and initial it.

♦ If you want to list additional information in the book, add as many pages as you need; this will personalize the book for your life situation.

♦ For added security, scan completed pages and important documents onto a computer disk or a memory stick.

♦ If your handwriting is illegible, type the answers on the CD-ROM included.

♦ Consult legal and financial advisors—this book does not replace their advice.

♦ Bring your book or computer file out of its safe location when paying bills and doing desk work. This will give you an opportunity to fill in the book or update changes.

Congratulations on deciding to get your affairs in order, and good luck! Your family and friends will thank you.

All About You

THIS SECTION LISTS INFORMATION you might need daily; for example, your Medicare number and Social Security number, etc. It also includes most of the information needed to complete your death certificate; that is, number of years in the county, education, your employer, kind of business, number of years in your occupation. You will also need information about your parents, which you can record in the family section that follows. For those who are retired, fill in this section with information about the employment you had for most of your life.

PERSONAL INFORMATION

Date Compiled: _____   Revised: _____

Name: _____

Aliases: _____

Name of Spouse, Domestic Partner, or Significant Other: _____

Mailing Address: _____

_____

Street Address: _____

_____

Phone Number(s): _____

Fax Number: _____   Cell Phone: _____

E-mail address: _____

Location of computer password: _____

Location of house keys: _____

Date of birth: _____   Place of birth: _____

Location of immunization records: _____

Number of years in county: _____

Education (highest degree / level of school completed): _____

Employer: _____

Type of business: _____

Number of years in occupation: _____

Location of medical records: _____

Blood type: _____

Allergies: _____

Medical conditions: _____

Location of your list of medications or box of meds:

Do you have a safe?   YES   NO   *If yes, have you told the appropriate person(s) about the location, contents, and combination?*   YES   NO

Name of person:

Location of storage unit and location of key:

If the unit has an entry code, what is the code?

Location of current income tax files:

Past files:

Location of airline miles (frequent flyer) paperwork:

Other items you want to list that are specific to the circumstances of your life:

FAMILY INFORMATION

As mentioned previously, the information about your parents in the first part of this section is needed to complete your death certificate. The rest is general family information. Feel free to add other topics to this section, such as names and birth dates of grandchildren, social security numbers of family members, and memories of family, etc.

PARENTS

MOTHER

First Name: _____ Middle: _____ Last (Maiden): _____

Date of Birth: _____ Birth State / Country: _____

Address: _____

_____

Phone Number: _____ Cell Phone: _____

E-mail Address: _____

FATHER

First Name: _____ Middle: _____ Last: _____

Date of Birth: _____ Birth State / Country: _____

Address: _____

_____

Phone Number: _____ Cell Phone: _____

E-mail Address: _____

SIBLINGS

1. Name: _____ Date of Birth: _____

Address: _____

_____

Phone Number: _____ Cell Phone: _____

E-mail Address: _____

2. Name: _____   Date of Birth: _____

Address: _____

_____

Phone Number: _____   Cell Phone: _____

E-mail Address: _____

3. Name: _____   Date of Birth: _____

Address: _____

_____

Phone Number: _____   Cell Phone: _____

E-mail Address: _____

4. Name: _____   Date of Birth: _____

Address: _____

_____

Phone Number: _____   Cell Phone: _____

E-mail Address: _____

5. Name: _____   Date of Birth: _____

Address: _____

_____

Phone Number: _____   Cell Phone: _____

E-mail Address: _____

6. Name: _____   Date of Birth: _____

Address: _____

_____

Phone Number: _____   Cell Phone: _____

E-mail Address: _____

CHILDREN

1. Name: _____   Date of Birth: _____

Address: _____

_____

Phone Number: _____   Cell Phone: _____

E-mail Address: _____

Social Security #: _____

2. Name: _____   Date of Birth: _____

Address: _____

_____

Phone Number: _____   Cell Phone: _____

E-mail Address: _____

Social Security #: _____

3. Name: _____   Date of Birth: _____

Address: _____

_____

Phone Number: _____   Cell Phone: _____

E-mail Address: _____

Social Security #: _____

4. Name: _____   Date of Birth: _____

Address: _____

_____

Phone Number: _____   Cell Phone: _____

E-mail Address: _____

Social Security #: _____

If there is other information you want your family to know about, use additional sheets of paper and add them to this book.

PETS

List any pets you have and any information that you want others to know about. For example, type of pet, name, location of medical records, medicines that they are taking, pedigree papers, and specific plans you have for them after you are deceased, etc.

IMPORTANT CONTACTS

DOCTORS (M.D., D.D., O.D., et al):

1. Name: _____ Specialty: _____

Address: _____

_____

Phone Number: _____ Fax Number: _____

Cell Phone: _____ E-mail Address: _____

2. Name: _____ Specialty: _____

Address: _____

_____

Phone Number: _____ Fax Number: _____

Cell Phone: _____ E-mail Address: _____

3. Name: _____ Specialty: _____

Address: _____

_____

Phone Number: _____ Fax Number: _____

Cell Phone: _____ E-mail Address: _____

4. Name: _____ Specialty: _____

Address: _____

_____

Phone Number: _____ Fax Number: _____

Cell Phone: _____ E-mail Address: _____

Primary Hospital/Clinic

Name:

Address:

Phone Number: *Fax Number:*

Cell Phone: *E-mail Address:*

Billing Office number:

Pharmacy

Name:

Address:

Phone Number: *Fax Number:*

Cell Phone: *E-mail Address:*

Lawyer(s)

1. Name:

Address:

Phone Number: *Fax Number:*

Cell Phone: *E-mail Address:*

2. Name:

Address:

Phone Number: *Fax Number:*

Cell Phone: *E-mail Address:*

3. Name:

Address:

Phone Number: *Fax Number:*

Cell Phone: *E-mail Address:*

ACCOUNTANT

Name:

Address:

Phone Number: *Fax Number:*

Cell Phone: *E-mail Address:*

VETERINARIAN

Name:

Address:

Phone Number: *Fax Number:*

Cell Phone: *E-mail Address:*

OTHER PEOPLE WHO ARE ACTIVELY IN YOUR LIFE

Name: *Phone Number:*

Name: *Phone Number:*

Name: *Phone Number:*

Name: *Phone Number:*

Name: *Phone Number:*

Name: *Phone Number:*

Name: *Phone Number:*

Name: *Phone Number:*

Religious Affiliation

Services attended at:

Name of Leader:

Address:

Phone Number: *Fax Number:*

Cell Phone: *E-mail Address:*

Military Service

Branch of Service:

Date Enlisted / Drafted: *Date Released:*

Serial / Service Number: *VA File #:*

Rank:

Location of Military Records, including your DD-214 Separation Document / Discharge Papers, and Disabled Veteran Paperwork, etc.:

See Resources (page 113) for Department of Veterans' Affairs and American Veterans Institute contact information.

Memberships

List your Club Memberships: Religious, Athletic/Health, Lodges/Fraternal Organizations, Automobile, Book, Collegiate, Community, Social, and location of records.

CHARITIES SUPPORTED

List the charities you support on a regular basis, as well as endowments and bequests you have made or have promised to make. Include amounts, pertinent dates, and contact information, etc. We often become confused about the last time we donated; this is a way to track your contributions so you don't duplicate them.

SUBSCRIPTIONS

List all subscriptions to newspapers, magazines, newsletters, journals, and radio and TV stations. The renewal date can usually be found on the mailing labels.

1. Subscription Name:

Renewal Date:

Length of renewal:

2. Subscription Name:

Renewal Date:

Length of renewal:

3. Subscription Name:

Renewal Date:

Length of renewal:

4. Subscription Name:

Renewal Date:

Length of renewal:

5. Subscription Name:

Renewal Date:

Length of renewal:

6. Subscription Name:

Renewal Date:

Length of renewal:

7. Subscription Name:

Renewal Date:

Length of renewal:

ALL THAT STUFF

Are there special items (a painting, bowl, vase, quilt, or book, etc.) that you want a certain person to have? If you have a will, each item needs to be listed and the recipient named. If you have a trust, you can make a note of that future gift here and sign this page. Whenever possible, describe the item. Also, put the person's name on the item if possible. Consult your lawyer about documenting the existence of this list for your trust. If such documentation does not happen, the list is null and void. Alternatively, you can give the item to the person while you're still alive.

Item 1:

Location of item:

Intended Recipient:

Your Signature: Date:

Item 2:

Location of item:

Intended Recipient:

Your Signature: Date:

Item 3:

Location of item:

Intended Recipient:

Your Signature: Date:

Item 4:

Location of item:

Intended Recipient:

Your Signature: Date:

Item 5:

Location of item:

Intended Recipient:

Your Signature: Date:

Items for Charity

Are there items that you want to go to a charity or organization? For example, books to go to the local library, or clothing/bedding to go to the local shelter. List those items and where you want them to go. If possible, include the address, phone number, and contact person of each organization on a separate piece of paper.

Item(s):

Name of charity/organization:

Item(s):

Name of charity/organization:

Item(s):

Name of charity/organization:

Item(s):

Name of charity/organization:

Item(s):

Name of charity/organization:

Item(s):

Name of charity/organization:

Item(s):

Name of charity/organization:

Item(s):

Name of charity/organization:

Item(s):

Name of charity/organization:

Item(s):

Name of charity/organization:

HIDING PLACES

While visiting her father's shop one afternoon at closing time, Claire, a friend of mine, helped her dad shut down, closing blinds, straightening up counters, and counting the money. When all was done, Claire watched in amazement as her father, who was in his mid-sixties, took a stepladder from the hallway, and, gathering up the money from the cash register, proceeded to lift a ceiling panel and stash the day's receipts in the ceiling. Momentarily speechless with surprise, Claire finally asked, "Dad, who else knows that your money is there?"

"Now *you* do," he replied.

Are there items in hiding places in your home? What items are hidden and where are they? Do you have any plans for them? If so, write them here.

DOCUMENTS ON FILE

This section includes the legal documents that you should have in place before your death or incapacitation. If you haven't considered all or any of these, it's a good idea to consult an attorney. You should review these documents every five years or when you make any changes. Put the original documents in a safe place, and put a copy with this book.

WILL

A will is a legal document specifying who gets your property or estate when you die. A will usually goes through probate, which is a legal process by which the court oversees the distribution of property left in the will.

Locations of Will(s):

Date of Will (or latest revision):

Attorney who Drafted Will:

Address:

Phone Number: *Fax Number:*

Cell Phone: *E-mail Address:*

EXECUTOR(S)

1. Name:

Address:

Phone Number: *Fax Number:*

Cell Phone: *E-mail Address:*

2. Name:

Address:

Phone Number: *Fax Number:*

Cell Phone: *E-mail Address:*

LIVING TRUST

There are many kinds of trusts. Discussed here is the living trust. For more information on other kinds of trusts, consult a lawyer. A living trust is a legal document controlling the transfer of property / assets in the trust when you die. It is set up while you are still alive and is considered revocable because you can change or revoke any part of it before you die. Living trusts avoid probate and allow property to be transferred promptly to heirs and beneficiaries.

Location of Trust:

Date of Trust (or latest revision):

Attorney who Drafted Trust:

Address:

Phone Number: *Fax Number:*

Cell Phone: *E-mail Address:*

TRUSTEE(S)

I. Name:

Address:

Phone Number: *Fax Number:*

Cell Phone: *E-mail Address:*

2. Name:

Address:

Phone Number: *Fax Number:*

Cell Phone: *E-mail Address:*

OTHER TRUSTS

1. Type of Trust:

Location of Trust:

Date of Trust (or last revision):

Attorney who Drafted Trust:

Address:

Phone Number: *Fax Number:*

Cell Phone: *E-mail Address:*

Trustee Name:

Address:

Phone Number: *Fax Number:*

Cell Phone: *E-mail Address:*

2. Type of Trust:

Location of Trust:

Date of Trust (or last revision):

Attorney who Drafted Trust:

Address:

Phone Number: *Fax Number:*

Cell Phone: *E-mail Address:*

Trustee Name:

Address:

Phone Number: *Fax Number:*

Cell Phone: *E-mail Address:*

Pourover Will

A pourover or backup will is the legal document that backs up a trust. If real/personal property does not get placed in your living trust, a pourover will would catch that property and ensure that it goes to whomever you want to have it.

Locations of Document(s):

Date of Document (or latest revision):

Attorney who drafted will:

Address:

Phone Number: *Fax Number:*

Cell Phone: *E-mail Address:*

Executor(s)

1. Name:

Address:

Phone Number: *Fax Number:*

Cell Phone: *E-mail Address:*

2. Name:

Address:

Phone Number: *Fax Number:*

Cell Phone: *E-mail Address:*

BENEFICIARY

Are you a beneficiary of a trust?   YES   NO

If yes, do you have power of appointment?   YES   NO

1. Name on Trust:

Location of Trust Paperwork:

2. Name on Trust:

Location of Trust Paperwork:

TRUSTOR/EXECUTOR

Are you a trustor or executor on someone else's trust or will?   YES   NO.
If yes, record that person's name and contact information.

1. Name:

Address:

Phone Number: *Fax Number:*

Cell Phone: *E-mail Address:*

2. Name:

Address:

Phone Number: *Fax Number:*

Cell Phone: *E-mail Address:*

3. Name:

Address:

Phone Number: *Fax Number:*

Cell Phone: *E-mail Address:*

DURABLE POWER OF ATTORNEY FOR HEALTH CARE/FIVE WISHES

These three documents do the same thing: they outline your wishes for healthcare, and intervention if you become unable to speak for yourself, and ask you to designate a healthcare agent to act on your behalf. The choice of documents is yours, but it is very important to have one of them in place. The Durable Power of Attorney for Health Care (DPAHC) is obtained from a lawyer and covers the basics: do you want everything done to keep you alive, or nothing, or something in between. The Advanced Directive, which can be obtained from your hospital, is more user friendly and gives you more opportunity to express your wishes. The Five Wishes addresses the topic from a personal, emotional, and spiritual place and is currently legal in thirty-seven states (the other documents are legal in every state). You'll find information on how to obtain a copy of Five Wishes in the resources at the back of this book.

Type of Document: *Date of Document (or latest revision):*

Location of Document(s):

Health Care Agent:

Address:

Phone Number: *Fax Number:*

Cell Phone: *E-mail Address:*

Alternative Agents

1. Name:

Address:

Phone Number: *Fax Number:*

Cell Phone: *E-mail Address:*

2. Name:

Address:

Phone Number: *Fax Number:*

Cell Phone: *E-mail Address:*

POWER OF ATTORNEY FOR FINANCIAL MATTERS OR ASSET MANAGEMENT

A Power of Attorney is a legal document in which you designate another person(s) to make financial decisions for you. There are many types of Powers of Attorney, such as general, swinging, limited, and durable. Each has a specific purpose and time when it can be used. If this document is not in place and you become incapacitated, a judge chooses who will act on your behalf. It is advantageous to name someone you trust to act in this capacity. See a lawyer to set this up.

Type of Power of Attorney:

Location of Document:

Date of Document (or latest revision):   *Expiration date:*

Attorney who Drafted Document:

Agent:

Name:

Address:

Phone Number: *Fax Number:*

Cell Phone: *E-mail Address:*

Type of Power of Attorney:

Location of Document:

Date of Document (or latest revision):   *Expiration date:*

Attorney who Drafted Document:

Agent:

Name:

Address:

Phone Number: *Fax Number:*

Cell Phone: *E-mail Address:*

Pre-hospital Do Not Resuscitate (DNR)

This is a form that can be obtained from a hospital or doctor's office. It allows you to instruct emergency medical personnel to forgo resuscitation in the event of cardiopulmonary arrest in pre-hospital settings, for example, your home, a long-term care facility, etc. This includes chest compressions, assisted ventilation, endotracheal intubation, defibrillation, and cardiotonic drugs.

Warning: Think seriously about putting this form in place, and speak with your doctor about the ramifications.

Date of Document (or latest revision): _____

❑ *A copy is at home (inform family and friends)*

Location at home: _____

❑ *A copy is at hospital / with 911*

❑ *A copy is with primary doctor (name):* _____

Other Legal Documents Not Already Listed

List name, location of document, and pertinent information, e.g. oral / written contracts, premarital agreements, long-term commitments, and documents you have cosigned, etc.

_____

_____

_____

_____

_____

_____

_____

_____

All About the Money

GO THROUGH EACH ACCOUNT and list the appropriate information requested. If there is additional information that you want listed, insert additional pages. If the information changes, insert new pages and remove any outdated information. Include PIN numbers when appropriate.

The important thing is for your family to be aware that an account exists. I heard a story about the actor Groucho Marx and his bank accounts. Groucho's heirs estimated that he had hundreds of accounts, but because they didn't have any record of most of them, they were out of luck: no record, no access to the accounts, which were worth millions of dollars! Unclaimed, the money reverts to the state. If you think there are unclaimed accounts, contact the treasurer's office of the state where the accounts, real estate, or other assets were held / owned.

BANKS AND CREDIT UNIONS

ACCOUNTS

Bank #1

Bank / Credit Union Name:

Address:

Phone Number: *Fax Number:*

Branch Number: *Contact Person:*

Type of Account(s):   *Account Number(s):*

Location of Bank Records:

Location of Checkbook:

Joint Account: YES   NO

Account Holder(s) in Addition to Yourself

1. Name:

Address:

Phone Number: *Fax Number:*

Cell Phone: *E-mail Address:*

Social Security Number:

2. Name:

Address:

Phone Number: *Fax Number:*

Cell Phone: *E-mail Address:*

Social Security Number:

Bank #2

Bank / Credit Union Name:

Address:

Phone Number: *Fax Number:*

Branch Number: *Contact Person:*

Type of Account(s):   *Account Number(s):*

Location of Bank Records:

Location of Checkbook:

Joint Account: YES   NO

Account Holder(s) in Addition to Yourself

1. Name:

Address:

Phone Number: *Fax Number:*

Cell Phone: *E-mail Address:*

Social Security Number:

2. Name:

Address:

Phone Number: *Fax Number:*

Cell Phone: *E-mail Address:*

Social Security Number:

Bank #3

Bank / Credit Union Name:

Address:

Phone Number: *Fax Number:*

Branch Number: *Contact Person:*

Type of Account(s):   *Account Number(s):*

Location of Bank Records:

Location of Checkbook:

Joint Account: YES   NO

Account Holder(s) in Addition to Yourself

1. Name:

Address:

Phone Number: *Fax Number:*

Cell Phone: *E-mail Address:*

Social Security Number:

2. Name:

Address:

Phone Number: *Fax Number:*

Cell Phone: *E-mail Address:*

Social Security Number:

Safe-deposit Boxes

Safe-deposit Box #1

Bank / Credit Union Name:

Address:

Phone Number: Fax Number:

Key #:

Location of key # 1:

Location of key # 2:

Authorized Signatures in Addition to Yourself

1. Name:

Address:

Phone Number: Fax Number:

Cell Phone: E-mail Address:

2. Name:

Address:

Phone Number: Fax Number:

Cell Phone: E-mail Address:

List contents of safety deposit box:

Safe-deposit Box #2

Bank / Credit Union Name:

Address:

Phone Number: *Fax Number:*

Key #:

Location of key #1:

Location of key #2:

Authorized Signatures in Addition to Yourself:

1. Name:

Address:

Phone Number: *Fax Number:*

Cell Phone: *E-mail Address:*

2. Name:

Address:

Phone Number: *Fax Number:*

Cell Phone: *E-mail Address:*

List contents of safety deposit box:

AUTO-PAY DEPOSITS AND ANNUITIES

(Check your credit-card statements and bank statements for up-to-date information.)

1. Source:

   Account #:

   Deposited to:

2. Source:

   Account #:

   Deposited to:

3. Source:

   Account #:

   Deposited to:

4. Source:

   Account #:

   Deposited to:

5. Source:

   Account #:

   Deposited to:

6. Source:

   Account #:

   Deposited to:

7. Source:

   Account #:

   Deposited to:

AUTO-PAY BILLS AND TRANSFERS

(Check your credit-card statements and bank statements for up-to-date information.)

Name of company:

    Date withdrawn:

    Credit Card / Bank:

Name of company:

    Date withdrawn:

    Credit Card / Bank:

Name of company:

    Date withdrawn:

    Credit Card / Bank:

Name of company:

    Date withdrawn:

    Credit Card / Bank:

Name of company:

    Date withdrawn:

    Credit Card / Bank:

Name of company:

    Date withdrawn:

    Credit Card / Bank:

Name of company:

    Date withdrawn:

    Credit Card / Bank:

INCOME/REVENUE

List types of income and location of all records. Income could include the following: current employment (not self-employment—use the business section for that), military and government benefits, pensions, trust funds, Social Security benefits, workers' compensation, disability, alimony, child support, rental income, payments from loans/promissory notes, copyrights, patent royalties, etc.

Type of Income	Amount	Frequency Pd.	End Date

CREDIT CARDS

Include credit cards, debit cards, ATM cards, department store cards, etc. It's a good idea to copy the contents of your wallet in case of theft. Keep the copies in a safe place, such as your safe-deposit box or in this book.

Location of credit card records:

Location of Credit Report:

Credit Card Protection Company:

Account Number:

Phone Number:

Card #1

Company / Type of card:

Address:

Phone Number:

Card Number:

Name on card:

Authorized Users:

Location of card:

Card #2

Company / Type of card:

Address:

Phone Number:

Card Number:

Name on card:

Authorized Users:

Location of card:

Card #3

Company / Type of card:

Address:

Phone Number:

Card Number:

Name on card:

Authorized Users:

Location of card:

Card #4

Company / Type of card:

Address:

Phone Number:

Card Number:

Name on card:

Authorized Users:

Location of card:

Card #5

Company / Type of card:

Address:

Phone Number:

Card Number:

Name on card:

Authorized Users:

Location of card:

INVESTMENTS

If you have more than two financial advisors and/or stockbrokers, photocopy this page before filling it out. List additional advisors/brokers on the photocopies, and then include them with this page. Use additional pages to include other important information about any of these.

Financial Advisor or Stockbroker #1

Name:

Company Name:

Address:

Phone Number: *Fax Number:*

Cell Phone: *E-mail Address:*

Account #1:

Account #2:

Account #3:

Financial Advisor or Stockbroker #2

Name:

Company Name:

Address:

Phone Number: *Fax Number:*

Cell Phone: *E-mail Address:*

Account #1:

Account #2;

Account #3:

MUTUAL FUNDS

If you have more than three mutual funds, photocopy this page before filling it out. List additional mutual funds on the photocopies, and then include them with this page. If there are beneficiaries for these accounts, please list their names and contact information. If investments are held by a broker, write "contact broker" wherever appropriate.

Mutual Fund #1

Name of Fund:

Held by:

Name on Account:

Type / Symbol: *# of purchased shares:*

Purchase Price: *Purchase Date:*

Location of investment records:

Mutual Fund #2

Name of Fund:

Held by:

Name on Account:

Type / Symbol: *# of purchased shares:*

Purchase Price: *Purchase Date:*

Location of investment records:

Mutual Fund #3

Name of Fund:

Held by:

Name on Account:

Type / Symbol: *# of purchased shares:*

Purchase Price: *Purchase Date:*

Location of investment records:

Stocks

Stock #1

Name of Company:

Name on Account:

Type / Symbol: # of Shares:

Purchase Price: Purchase Date:

Location of stock certificate: ❑ with broker in personal files

Stock #2

Name of Company:

Name on Account:

Type / Symbol: # of Shares:

Purchase Price: Purchase Date:

Location of stock certificate: ❑ with broker in personal files

Stock #3

Name of Company:

Name on Account:

Type / Symbol: # of Shares:

Purchase Price: Purchase Date:

Location of stock certificate: ❑ with broker in personal files

Stock #4

Name of Company:

Name on Account:

Type / Symbol: # of Shares:

Purchase Price: Purchase Date:

Location of stock certificate: ❑ with broker in personal files

Stock #5

Name of Company:

Name on Account:

Type / Symbol: # of Shares:

Purchase Price: Purchase Date:

Location of stock certificate: ❑ with broker in personal files

Stock #6

Name of Company:

Name on Account:

Type / Symbol: # of Shares:

Purchase Price: Purchase Date:

Location of stock certificate: ❑ with broker in personal files

Stock #7

Name of Company:

Name on Account:

Type / Symbol: # of Shares:

Purchase Price: Purchase Date:

Location of stock certificate: ❑ with broker in personal files

Stock #8

Name of Company:

Name on Account:

Type / Symbol: # of Shares:

Purchase Price: Purchase Date:

Location of stock certificate: ❑ with broker in personal files

U.S. Savings Bonds

1. Name on Bond:

Serial Number: *Issue Date:*

Location of Bond:

2. Name on Bond:

Serial Number: *Issue Date:*

Location of Bond:

3. Name on Bond:

Serial Number: *Issue Date:*

Location of Bond:

4. Name on Bond:

Serial Number: *Issue Date:*

Location of Bond:

5. Name on Bond:

Serial Number: *Issue Date:*

Location of Bond:

6. Name on Bond:

Serial Number: *Issue Date:*

Location of Bond:

7. Name on Bond:

Serial Number: *Issue Date:*

Location of Bond:

8. Name on Bond:

Serial Number: *Issue Date:*

Location of Bond:

ANNUITIES

If you have more than two annuities, photocopy this page before you fill it out. List additional annuities on the photocopied pages and include them with this page.

Annuity #1

Name of Company: _____

Address: _____

_____

Phone Number: _____

Owner: _____

Policy Number: _____ Value: _____

Beneficiary: _____

Location of Paperwork: _____

Annuity #2

Name of Company: _____

Address: _____

_____

Phone Number: _____

Owner: _____

Policy Number: _____ Value: _____

Beneficiary: _____

Location of Paperwork: _____

IRAs

IRA #1

Name of Holder: _____

Name of Owner: _____

Beneficiary: _____

Account Number: _____ Type: _____

Location of paperwork: _____

IRA #2

Name of Holder:

Name of Owner:

Beneficiary:

Account Number: Type:

Location of paperwork:

IRA #3

Name of Holder:

Name of Owner:

Beneficiary:

Account Number: Type:

Location of paperwork:

IRA #4

Name of Holder:

Name of Owner:

Beneficiary:

Account Number: Type:

Location of paperwork:

IRA #5

Name of Holder:

Name of Owner:

Beneficiary:

Account Number: Type:

Location of paperwork:

Profit Sharing and Pensions

1. Name of Plan: _____

Beneficiaries: _____

Whom to Contact: _____

Location of Records: _____

2. Name of Plan: _____

Beneficiaries: _____

Whom to Contact: _____

Location of Records: _____

3. Name of Plan: _____

Beneficiaries: _____

Whom to Contact: _____

Location of Records: _____

4. Name of Plan: _____

Beneficiaries: _____

Whom to Contact: _____

Location of Records: _____

5. Name of Plan: _____

Beneficiaries: _____

Whom to Contact: _____

Location of Records: _____

6. Name of Plan: _____

Beneficiaries: _____

Whom to Contact: _____

Location of Records: _____

REAL ESTATE

This section allows space for your primary home, secondary home (e.g., holiday home, or retirement home, etc.), and rental property. Photocopy this page and the next and complete them for each property you own. (Remember to photocopy before filling them out!) If you have more than three homes, insert additional photocopied pages. If you have home security measures in place, include information about them; for example, safes, gates, and alarm systems. Record combinations, locations of keys and/or passwords, and location(s) of relevant records.

PRIMARY HOME

Name(s) on Title:

Address:

Assessor's Parcel #:   *County:*

Location of deed, title, closing papers, appraisals:

How is the property held (e.g., joint tenancy)?

Bank/Mortgage Company (if applicable):

Name:

Address:

Contact Person:

Phone Number: *Fax Number:*

Cell Phone: *E-mail Address:*

Loan Number:

Location of Mortgage Papers:

Seconds on the property:

Liens on the property:

Amount: $

Name of Lien Holder:

Address:

Phone Number: Fax Number:

Cell Phone: E-mail Address:

Location of Lien Holder Records:

Are property taxes current?   YES   NO   Due Date:

Location of Tax Records:

Names and phone numbers of adjacent property owners (use additional paper if needed):

If on a rural right of way or easement, is there a road-maintenance agreement?
If yes, has it been recorded?   YES   NO

Location of agreement:

Location of improvement / repair records, especially roof repair, water system, plot plans, maps and surveys, architectural drawings and any other relevant documents, including contracts with contractors, service agreements, warranties, etc.

Other information not already listed, including names, addresses and phone numbers of people who render services at your home — housecleaner, chimney sweep, landscaper / gardener, pool maintenance, alarm company, etc. (use additional paper if necessary):

SECONDARY HOME

If you have additional homes, photocopy this section and complete it for each home. If you have home security measures in place, include information about them; for example, safes, gates, and alarm systems. Record combinations, locations of keys and/or passwords, and location(s) of relevant records.

Name(s) on Title:

Address:

Assessor's Parcel #:   *County:*

Location of deed, title, closing papers, appraisals:

How is the property held (e.g., joint tenancy)?

Bank/Mortgage Company (if applicable):

Name:

Address:

Contact Person:

Phone Number: *Fax Number:*

Cell Phone: *E-mail Address:*

Loan Number:

Location of Mortgage Papers:

Seconds on the property:

Liens on the property:

Amount: $

Name of Lien Holder:

Address:

Phone Number: *Fax Number:*

Cell Phone: *E-mail Address:*

Location of Lien Holder Records:

Are property taxes current?   YES   NO   Due:

Location of Tax Records:

Names, phone numbers of adjacent property owners (use additional paper if needed):

If on a rural right of way or easement, is there a road-maintenance agreement? If yes, has it been recorded?   YES   NO

Location of Agreement:

Location of improvement / repair records, especially roof repair, water system, plot plans, maps and surveys, architectural drawings and any other relevant documents, including contracts with contractors, service agreements, warranties, etc.

Other information not already listed, including names, addresses and phone numbers of people who render services at your home — housecleaner, chimney sweep, landscaper / gardener, pool maintenance, alarm company, etc. (use additional paper if necessary):

RENTAL PROPERTY

Name(s) on Title:

Address:

Assessor's Parcel #:   County:

Location of deed, title, closing papers, appraisals:

How is the property held (e.g., joint tenancy)?

Bank / Mortgage Company (if applicable):

Name:

Address:

Contact Person:

Phone Number: Fax Number:

Cell Phone: E-mail Address:

Loan Number:

Location of Mortgage Papers:

Seconds on the property:

Liens on the property:

Amount: $

Name of Lien Holder:

Address:

Phone Number: Fax Number:

Cell Phone: E-mail Address:

Location of Lien Holder Records:

Are property taxes current?   YES   NO   Due:

Location of Tax Records:

Names, phone numbers of adjacent property owners (use additional paper if needed):

If on a rural right of way or easement, is there a road-maintenance agreement? If yes, has it been recorded?   YES   NO

Location of agreement:

Location of improvement / repair records, especially roof repair, water system, plot plans, maps and surveys, architectural drawings and any other relevant documents, including contracts with contractors, service agreements, warranties, etc.

Other information not already listed, including names, addresses and phone numbers of people who render services at your home — housecleaner, chimney sweep, landscaper / gardener, pool maintenance, alarm company, etc. (use additional paper if necessary):

Rental is ❑ *Long-term*   ❑ *Vacation*   ❑ *Other*

Who manages the rental?

Name:

Address:

Phone Number: *Fax Number:*

Cell Phone: *E-mail Address:*

Current Tenant:

Phone Number: *Fax Number:*

Cell Phone: *E-mail Address:*

Rent: *Due Date:*

Move-in Date:

Amount Deposited for First and Last: $ *Cleaning:* $

Location of Rental Agreement:

Utility payment agreement (if not stated in the rental agreement):

Who owns the refrigerator?

stove?

washer/dryer?

If there is a photo record or videotape of property, where is it located?

If you want to say more about the rental (e.g., history of rent increases, nature of relationship with tenants, location of appliance warranties and instructions, location of repair and improvement receipts, location or particularities of utilities, etc.), use an additional sheet of paper and attach it to this page.

Use a separate sheet of paper to show improvements on your properties, locating septic system, alarm systems, gas and water lines, sprinkler systems, and breaker boxes with labeled breakers, etc. Include water, gas, and electrical shutoff valves. If there are special instructions, such as water or pool treatment instructions, please list them and the location of the instructions. Also list names and phone numbers of people who work on the property: plumber, electrician, chimney sweep, gardener, and housekeeper, etc. Remember to keep receipts for all improvements made.

RENTED PROPERTY
(complete this section only if you live in rented property)

Property Owner / Landlord:

Name:

Address:

Phone Number: Fax Number:

Cell Phone: E-mail Address:

Rent: Due Date:

Did you pay a deposit? YES NO If yes, amount: $

For what (first / last month's rent, cleaning, pet)?

Location of rental agreement:

Describe utility-payment agreement (if not stated on rent agreement):

If you have photos of the rental, where are they located?

What else do you want to say about the rental (e.g., history of rent increases, nature of relationship with landlord, location of appliance warranties and instructions, location of repair and improve-ment receipts, and location or particularities of utilities, etc.)?

Other Assets

Vehicles

If you own more than two vehicles, photocopy this page, write the information about them on the copies, and include them with this page.

Type of Vehicle and ID Number:

Model: *Year:*

Location (boat in marina or in storage unit, etc.):

Location of maintenance records, location of keys and hide-a-key, security systems, photos of vehicle, and any specific information others should know about the vehicle(s).

Type of Vehicle and ID Number:

Model: *Year:*

Location (boat in marina or in storage unit, etc.):

Location of maintenance records, location of keys and hide-a-key, security systems, photos of vehicle, and any specific information others should know about the vehicle(s).

Type of Vehicle and ID Number:

Model: *Year:*

Location (boat in marina or in storage unit, etc.):

Location of maintenance records, location of keys and hide-a-key, security systems, photos of vehicle, and any specific information others should know about the vehicle(s).

ANTIQUES

Location, value, location of appraisals, appraisers used, date last appraised, and any other information others should know about antiques.

INTELLECTUAL PROPERTY

Items that you produced: books, art, poetry, etc. Include what each item is, location of paperwork and records, and any other information you think is important for others to know. It's wise to have photos taken of artwork. If you are insured, contact your insurance company; they might have specific instructions about this.

OTHER (ART, LIBRARY, COLLECTIBLES)

List each asset, its location, value (if known), knowledgeable contact person, insurance company, location of paperwork, location of photos or videotape of asset. Do you anticipate receiving any viatical settlements?

LEGAL MATTERS

Write down pertinent information about lawsuits, claims, etc. that you are involved with. Include the location of the documents. Are you involved in any legal actions as a defendant or plaintiff? Are you going to be the recipient of any settlement / awards? Explain.

Loans

Items Loaned Out

Are there any items you have lent out to others that you want your family to know about? Write what each item is, who has it, its location, and any agreements relating to the loan.

Example: *My Steinway grand piano is on loan to Janet James (address and phone number) until I can fit it into my new home.*

MONEY OWED TO ME

Note: *If you have more than two loans, photocopy this page before you fill it out, use the blank photocopies to list additional loans, and include them with this page.*

THE FOLLOWING PEOPLE/COMPANIES OWE ME MONEY:

Loan #1

Person/Company Name:

Address:

Phone Number: Fax Number:

Cell Phone: E-mail Address:

Amount of loan: $ Interest rate:

Due date: Payment terms:

Collateral:

Location of loan agreement:

Loan #2

Person/Company Name:

Address:

Phone Number: Fax Number:

Cell Phone: E-mail Address:

Amount of loan: $ Interest rate:

Due date: Payment terms:

Collateral:

Location of loan agreement:

Loans that I owe
(other than mortgage, credit card, and business loans):

Note: *If you owe on more than two loans, photocopy this page before filling it out, use the blank photocopies to list additional loans, and include them with this page.*

Loan #1

Person / Company Name:

Address:

Phone Number: Fax Number:

Cell Phone: E-mail Address:

Amount of loan: $ Interest rate:

Due date: Payment terms:

Location of loan agreement:

Loan #2

Person / Company Name:

Address:

Phone Number: Fax Number:

Cell Phone: E-mail Address:

Amount of loan: $ Interest rate:

Due date: Payment terms:

Location of loan agreement:

COSIGNER OR GUARANTOR

Are you a cosigner or a guarantor on any loans?   *YES   NO*
If yes, fill in the following information:

Loan #1

Who is the cosigner, or whose loan did you guarantee?

Address:

Phone Number: *Fax Number:*

Cell Phone: *E-mail Address:*

Amount of loan: $ *Interest rate:*

Due date: *Payment terms:*

Location of loan agreement:

Loan #2

Who is the cosigner, or whose loan did you guarantee?

Address:

Phone Number: *Fax Number:*

Cell Phone: *E-mail Address:*

Amount of loan: $ *Interest rate:*

Due date: *Payment terms:*

Location of loan agreement:

Are You Covered?

KNOW YOUR INSURANCE COVERAGE

I WORKED FOR A CLIENT WHO, in addition to Medicare, had a supplemental insurance plan from her deceased husband's company. I assisted her with bill paying, setting up auto-pay, tracking medical insurance claims, balancing her checkbook, and organizing file cabinets, closets, and drawers. I decided that I wanted to know more about my client's supplemental insurance, and discovered that the plan had a drug benefit that my client hadn't known about. After many calls to the insurance company and the local pharmacy, I figured out how much money my client had already paid for medications at full price. With this information, the insurance company repaid her more than $3000 for the past year. They were able to go back only one year to reimburse my client, even though she hadn't put in a claim for five years. This resulted in her losing many thousands of dollars—and in my increased awareness of checking every client's insurance policies.

There are many kinds of insurance. The main ones are listed here, with space at the end to add information about other kinds if necessary or if you need additional space for a particular type of insurance. If there's additional information that you want your family to know, please add pages to explain. This book is more a location device than a place to put *all* the information. It's not a place for the actual policies, which need to be stored in a secure location.

HEALTH INSURANCE

Policy #1

Health Insurance Company:

Agent or Agency Name:

Address:

Phone Number: Fax Number:

Cell Phone: E-mail Address:

Policy Number: Type of Insurance:

Named insured:

Is there a drug benefit?   YES   NO

Deductible: $ Maximum out of pocket per year: $

Location of Policy:

Policy # 2

Health Insurance Company:

Agent or Agency Name:

Address:

Phone Number: Fax Number:

Cell Phone: E-mail Address:

Policy Number: Type of Insurance:

Named Insured:

Is there a drug benefit?   YES   NO

Deductible: $ Maximum out of pocket per year: $

Location of Policy:

Homeowner's or Renter's Insurance

Insurance Company Name:

Agent / Agency Name:

Address:

Phone Number: Fax Number:

Cell Phone: E-mail Address:

Policy Number: Type of Insurance:

Address of insured property (if different from primary residence):

Deductible: $

Type of Coverage: ❑ Fire   ❑ Flood   ❑ Earthquake

Other Coverage:

Liability: Amount: $

Amount the Property is Insured for: $

Location of policy, photos, video of property:

Rental Property Insurance

Insurance Company Name:

Agent / Agency Name:

Address:

Phone Number: Fax Number:

Cell Phone: E-mail Address:

Policy Number: Type of Insurance:

Address of insured property (if different from primary residence):

Deductible: $

Type of Coverage: ☐ Fire ☐ Flood ☐ Earthquake

Other Coverage:

Liability: Amount: $

Amount the property is insured for: $

Location of policy, photos, video of property:

Disability Insurance

Insurance Company Name:

Agent / Agency Name:

Address:

Phone Number: Fax Number:

Cell Phone: E-mail Address:

Policy Number:

Named Insured:

Waiting Period: Payout Amount: $ Duration:

Location of Policy:

Life Insurance

Policy #1

Insurance Company Name:

Agent / Agency Name:

Address:

Phone Number: Fax Number:

Cell Phone: E-mail Address:

Policy Number:

Named Insured:

Name of beneficiary(s):

Address:

Payout Amount: $

If you have taken out a loan against your life insurance:

Loan Amount: $

Location of Policy:

Policy #2

Insurance Company Name:

Agent/Agency Name:

Address:

Phone Number: *Fax Number:*

Cell Phone: *E-mail Address:*

Policy Number:

Named Insured:

Name of beneficiary(s):

Address:

Payout Amount: $

If you have taken out a loan against your life insurance:

Loan Amount: $

Location of Policy:

Vehicle Insurance
(automobile, motorcycle, boat, rv, snowmobile, airplane)

Policy #1

Owner of Vehicle:

Model / type of vehicle:

VIN number:

Insurance Company:

Agent / Agency Name:

Address:

Phone Number: Fax Number:

Cell Phone: E-mail Address:

Policy Number:

Location of Policy:

Policy #2

Owner of Vehicle:

Model / type of vehicle:

VIN number:

Insurance Company:

Agent / Agency Name:

Address:

Phone Number: Fax Number:

Cell Phone: E-mail Address:

Policy Number:

Location of Policy:

Policy #3

Owner of Vehicle:

Model / type of vehicle:

VIN number:

Insurance Company:

Agent / Agency Name:

Address:

Phone Number: Fax Number:

Cell Phone: E-mail Address:

Policy Number:

Location of Policy:

OTHER INSURANCE

Policy #1

Type of Insurance:

Insurance Company:

Agent / Agency Name:

Address:

Phone Number: Fax Number:

Cell Phone: E-mail Address:

Policy Number:

Location of Policy:

Policy #2

Type of Insurance:

Insurance Company:

Agent / Agency Name:

Address:

Phone Number: *Fax Number:*

Cell Phone: *E-mail Address:*

Policy Number:

Location of Policy:

Your Livelihood

EMPLOYMENT RECORD

COMPLETE THIS PAGE if you are employed; photocopy the page if you have more than one job.

My present employer is:

Job Title:

Location of Business:

Phone Number: Fax Number:

Cell Phone: E-mail Address:

Supervisor:

Date employment started:

Do you have benefits?   YES   NO

If yes, location of the benefit records:

Are you a union member?   YES   NO

If yes, name of local:

Location of union records:

Location of pay records:

Do you have a retirement program?   YES   NO

If yes, location of the retirement records:

Do you have a résumé?   YES   NO

If yes, location of the résumé:

Date last updated:

BUSINESS INFORMATION

Complete this section *only* if you are self-employed, are a partner, or a corporation. Some items will not pertain to you. There is a lot of flexibility in filling in what's pertinent to *your* business. If you have more than one business, photocopy the pages and fill in a separate one for each business.

Name of Business:

Owner's / Partner's Name(s):

Address:

Phone Number: *Fax Number:*

Cell Phone: *E-mail Address:*

Location of computer password:

How is the company held?

Sole Proprietor   *Partnership*   *Corporation*   *LLC*

If incorporated, list corporate officers:

Date of incorporation: *Corporation #:*

State incorporated:

Location of stock certificates:

Location of Partnership / Corporate Records:

List names of board of directors, titles, and contact information on a separate piece of paper.

Federal Taxpayer ID #:

State Employer ID #:

Dunn & Bradstreet #:

Licenses / permits (City / County Business, EPA #, Air Quality, etc.; include expiration dates):

Location of permits and licenses:

Resale Number:

Key Employees

1. Name: _____

Job / Title: _____

Phone Number: _____ *Fax Number:* _____

Cell Phone: _____ *E-mail Address:* _____

2. Name: _____

Job / Title: _____

Phone Number: _____ *Fax Number:* _____

Cell Phone: _____ *E-mail Address:* _____

Other Key People

Attorney: _____

Phone Number: _____ *Fax Number:* _____

Cell Phone: _____ *E-mail Address:* _____

Accountant / CPA: _____

Phone Number: _____ *Fax Number:* _____

Cell Phone: _____ *E-mail Address:* _____

Bookkeeper: _____

Phone Number: _____ *Fax Number:* _____

Cell Phone: _____ *E-mail Address:* _____

Computer Consultant: _____

Computer system used: _____

Location of Access Code: _____

Phone Number: _____ *Fax Number:* _____

Cell Phone: _____ *E-mail Address:* _____

Alarm company:

Phone Number: Fax Number:

Cell Phone: E-mail Address:

OTHER IMPORTANT INDIVIDUALS IN THE BUSINESS

1. Name:

Function:

Phone Number: Fax Number:

Cell Phone: E-mail Address:

2. Name:

Function:

Phone Number: Fax Number:

Cell Phone: E-mail Address:

3. Name:

Function:

Phone Number: Fax Number:

Cell Phone: E-mail Address:

4. Name:

Function:

Phone Number: Fax Number:

Cell Phone: E-mail Address:

5. Name:

Function:

Phone Number: Fax Number:

Cell Phone: E-mail Address:

BUSINESS BANKING

If you have more accounts than are listed below, photocopy this page, enter the information on the additional page(s), and include them with this page.

Account #1

Bank Name:

Address:

Contact Person:

Phone Number: *Fax Number:*

Cell Phone: *E-mail Address:*

Location of bank records:

Checking Account Number:

Name(s) on account:

Savings Account Number:

Name(s) on account:

Money Market Account:

Name(s) on account:

Certificate of Deposit:

Name(s) on account:

Line of Credit:

Safe-deposit Box?   YES   NO

If YES, Key #:   *Location:*

List contents of safe-deposit box on a separate sheet of paper and include it here.

Other information about account:

BUSINESS INSURANCE

LIABILITY INSURANCE

Insurance Company: _____ Agent / Agency: _____

Address: _____

_____

Phone Number: _____ Fax Number: _____

Cell Phone: _____ E-mail Address: _____

Policy Number: _____

Location of Policy: _____

GROUP HEALTH INSURANCE

Insurance Company: _____ Agent / Agency: _____

Address: _____

_____

Phone Number: _____ Fax Number: _____

Cell Phone: _____ E-mail Address: _____

Policy Number: _____

Location of Policy: _____

WORKERS' COMPENSATION INSURANCE

Insurance Company: _____ Agent / Agency: _____

Address: _____

_____

Phone Number: _____ Fax Number: _____

Cell Phone: _____ E-mail Address: _____

Policy Number: _____

Location of Policy: _____

Business Vehicle Insurance

Insurance Company: _____ Agent / Agency: _____

Address: _____

_____

Phone Number: _____ Fax Number: _____

Cell Phone: _____ E-mail Address: _____

Policy Number: _____

Location of Policy: _____

Business Property Insurance

Insurance Company: _____ Agent / Agency: _____

Address: _____

_____

Phone Number: _____ Fax Number: _____

Cell Phone: _____ E-mail Address: _____

Policy Number: _____

Location of Policy: _____

Directors'/Officers' Liability Insurance

Insurance Company: _____ Agent / Agency: _____

Address: _____

_____

Phone Number: _____ Fax Number: _____

Cell Phone: _____ E-mail Address: _____

Policy Number: _____

Location of Policy: _____

PRODUCT LIABILITY

Insurance Company: _____ *Agent / Agency:* _____

Address: _____

_____

Phone Number: _____ *Fax Number:* _____

Cell Phone: _____ *E-mail Address:* _____

Policy Number: _____

Location of Policy: _____

KEY MAN LIFE

Insurance Company: _____ *Agent / Agency:* _____

Address: _____

_____

Phone Number: _____ *Fax Number:* _____

Cell Phone: _____ *E-mail Address:* _____

Policy Number: _____

Location of Policy: _____

OTHER INSURANCE

Type of Insurance: _____

Insurance Company: _____ *Agent / Agency:* _____

Address: _____

_____

Phone Number: _____ *Fax Number:* _____

Cell Phone: _____ *E-mail Address:* _____

Policy Number: _____

Location of Policy: _____

Procedures and Policies

If there is an employee procedures and policies handbook / manual, where is it located?

Is there a benefits package or vacation policy for employees? Explain:

If others may need to know about any additional business information that you keep in your head or that is not easily locatable, write it on an additional sheet of paper and attach it here.

Have you ever filed for bankruptcy?   YES   NO

If yes, location of paperwork:

Are there outstanding loans? List separately: whom you owe, amount, terms, and any other information you want to include here.

Location of loan paperwork:

A Graceful Farewell

FINAL WISHES

FOR MOST OF US, ANY SERIOUS THOUGHT OF DEATH evokes a variety of emotions: sadness, fear, anxiety and curiosity. Some of us avoid the subject altogether. In the past few years much has been written about the subject. I believe that if we face death we can live more fully now (live more in the moment). This section gives you the opportunity to say how you want things to be when you are dying and after your death. Take some time to reflect on others in your life who have died and how you viewed their passing. Was there too much activity, or not enough? Were they alone? Was there chaos or calmness? Did the family/friends know what to do? Was there confusion? Were they at home or in the hospital? Then consider how you would want it to be for you.

Judith Redwing Keyssar is a friend and colleague of mine who works as a midwife to the dying. She is a registered nurse and works in oncology, critical care, home health, and hospice. Her organization, "Transformations," is listed in the resource section of this workbook. Currently Director of Patient Care Services at Zen Hospice Project in San Francisco, Redwing has this to say about the process of dying:

Death is the one journey that we will all take. We will all die, and we will all die differently. It is possible to die with dignity, grace, compassion, and awareness. That does not mean it will necessarily be easy or painless or without fear. Our fear of the unknown is huge, often so huge that people do not want to even begin the exploration of their own mortality. Most have not prepared themselves or their loved ones with ideas of how to assist them on this journey.

Being prepared is our simplest and most useful tool. Whatever you can do ahead of time makes everything easier when the time arrives for you to be lying in bed, letting go of every bit of earthly reality.

This opportunity to prepare for dying and death is available to all of us. There are books and workshops and people to talk to about this subject. The key is beginning the conversation. To prepare oneself for death, one must have thought about it ahead of time. You can talk to the people who might be helping you, comforting you, holding your hand, massaging your feet. You can let your medical practitioners know your wishes. You can have conversations with family and friends about your wishes—how you want your dying to be. It requires taking a long look into the mirror of mortality, and examining your own beliefs, values, dreams, and desires.

In this section you have an opportunity to be specific about your wishes. The more specific you can be, the less chance of confusion and upset later. Spare those left behind that worry and pressure, and state your desires below.

It *is* hard to die, and it will always be so, even when we have learned to accept death as an integral part of life, because dying means giving up life on this earth. But if we can learn to view death from a different perspective, to reintroduce it into our lives so that it comes not as a dreaded stranger but as an expected companion to our life, then we can also learn to live our lives with meaning—with full appreciation of our finiteness, of the limits on our time here.

— Elisabeth Kübler Ross, M. D., *Death: the Final Stage of Growth*

Accepting our Limitations

Today, end-of-life issues are being handled differently than in years past, yet are still extremely challenging. The choices are many. Options such as staying at home while aging, moving into a retirement community or home, living in a nursing home, living with children or friends, hiring caregivers to assist us, inviting hospice to assist, or signing up with a medical alarm company, are all available. Yet this does not mean that the individual decisions are any easier to make. Puzzling issues arise, such as where to live if your house is too big and you are no longer able to care for it; needing to be closer to medical support or family; feeling isolated because of losing your driver's license and being unable to get around as before; managing finances if you don't understand them and don't have the energy to figure them out. In addition, there might be emotional issues, such as not wanting to burden anyone, maintaining independence, and losing friends and family.

For children or loved ones, watching a parent go through this is worrisome. Questions such as where a parent should live, who cares for them and how it is paid for can cause incredible stress that adds to the difficult decisions needing to be made. There is a fine line between allowing a loved one their independence and taking over to protect them. Losing one's drivers license can throw an elder person into a depression that worsens their current medical state. And we want to make the best choices for our loved one or help him or her make the best choices.

Stating your intentions while you're still able will help your loved ones make important and difficult decisions later on. These wishes can't be set in stone and are not legally binding, because unforeseen circumstances may dictate other actions. Educating yourself about your options will give you more information on which to base informed choices. You'll also need to look at the cost-effectiveness and financial realities of your wishes. Possible choices include assisted living, skilled nursing homes, remaining at home with family / friends as caregivers, retirement communities, hiring caregivers, or moving in with family or friends. Choosing one of these options might assume a level of financial independence. Not everyone will be able to afford all of the options. Costs will vary depending on your needs and the type of care you choose. For example, in northern California in 2006, twenty-four-hour care in the home costs approximately $14,000 / month. In a shared room in a skilled nursing home, the cost ranges from $4,740 to $6,000 / month. In an assisted living facility, the range is $2,500 to $6,200 / month for a private living space. Having a family member care for us also costs indirectly in loss of income for the caregiver and potential emotional stress related to care-giving. These are big decisions that need discussion with those involved.

Talk with friends who've had to face these issues, and discuss this subject with your family. Research the Internet for organizations that can help you plan potential options, such as Medicare, National Citizens' Coalition for Nursing Home Reform, AARP, the National Center for Assisted Living, and the American Health Care Association. You can state your preferences in your Durable Power of Attorney for Health Care or Five Wishes. In choosing any of the above, it is not legally binding and will depend solely on the circumstances at the time.

If I am unable to care for myself, if my body is frail, or if I am unable to make decisions for myself, I want:

❑ *to stay at home with family, friends, loved ones (names):*

_____

_____

❑ *to move in with (name):* _____

❑ *to stay at home with caregivers*

❑ *to have hospice assist me and my family*

❑ *to move to a care facility; my first choice is:*

Name of facility: _____

Address of facility: _____

_____

Phone number: _____

Contact person: _____

Close to Death/At the Time of Death

Make sure your healthcare agent and other important people have the following information. It may seem funny to note where in the home you want to be, yet it can become an issue if not thought out. I worked with a family who wanted to have their mom die at home and have a home funeral. This family spent a lot of time in the kitchen. It was the center of the home. While the mother was sick, they moved her bed to a room off the kitchen so she could be a part of the activity. Mom enjoyed this very much. Then mom died and the family became uncomfortable about having her body so close to the heart of the house. They felt that it would have been better to have mom in another room and visit her when they felt the need. They eventually moved mom to another location and visited her there. They had a nice home funeral.

I want to (*check all the boxes that apply*):

❑ *be at home if at all possible.*
　Where in the home? _____

❑ *be in the hospital or in a medical facility*

❑ *be with my preferred family members (names):*

_____

❑ *be with my preferred friends (names):*

_____

❑ *hospice care*

❑ *be visited by my religious representative (name):*

❑ *other:* _____

I want the room (*check all that apply*):

❑ *to be serene*

❑ *to be a private place*

❑ *to be active, with people in and out*

❑ *to have the bed near a window*

❑ *to have candles burning*

❑ *to have singing*

❑ *to have music playing (specify type of music):* _____

❑ *other:* _____

AFTER DEATH

The following section includes some of the most important and sensitive work you will do. Taking the time now to write down your wishes will mean so much to the loved ones you leave behind. Even if you do not have family, someone will need to know how you want things handled. Write your thoughts here and tell those you have chosen to be responsible for making arrangements about this book and its location. Copy pertinent pages and give to those responsible. Put your funeral wishes in an accessible place, *not* in your safe deposit box, because it cannot be opened and read until after burial. If you want someone other than your next of kin to handle your arrangements, make sure you have completed your Five Wishes or Durable Power of Attorney for Health Care stating the name of the person doing the arranging (making the decisions). Many states now have Personal Preference Laws that allow you to write your wishes down, designating an agent for body disposition who can make decisions on your behalf. For a full list of states and their rules, go to Funeral Consumer's Alliance's webpage at www.funerals.org/pref.htm or call 800-765-0107. If there is no official, legal document in place, the next of kin will have to sign any paperwork needed or the county's public administrator will need to be contacted. Not having your wishes in writing can cause delay, upset, and needless stress. As you can imagine, this could be time consuming and emotionally difficult for those close to the deceased.

OPTIONS

You can choose from many options. There are full-service funerals, which include embalming and dressing of the deceased, viewing at the funeral home or other location such as a church, and transportation to the cemetery, entombment, or cremation site. The casket can be open or closed. "The average cost of a funeral, as of July 2004, is $6,500. That includes an outer burial container, but does not include cemetery costs." From the National Funeral Directors Association's web page, www.nfda.org. This fee includes the basic service fee—filing death certificates and other required permits, coordinating plans with the cemetery or crematory; and filing for Social Security, veterans, and insurance benefits. This fee may also include overhead costs such as insurance, advertising, taxes. Extras such as flowers, obituary notices, limousines, acknowledgments cards or clergy are not part of the basic service fee and could be priced in a package or separately.

Another option is a direct burial without embalming, a viewing or a funeral service. Sometimes there is a memorial service at the gravesite or held afterwards in a home, hall or church, but the mortuary is not involved. This costs less than a full-service funeral and includes the funeral home's basic service fee, care of the body and transportation, and purchase of the casket or burial container. The cemetery plot or crypt is separate. The cost could range from $725 to $1,600 in northern California. Call local mortuaries for price comparisons.

Direct cremation is another choice. There is no embalming, and the body is cremated shortly after death. There is no viewing, but a memorial service may be held at the family's convenience. The remains can be buried, scattered, kept at home or placed in a crypt. These services cost less than the full service funeral. In northern California, direct cremations cost between $840 and $1,600. This includes completing the necessary paperwork, transporting the body to the crematorium, cremation process, and returning the cremains to the funeral home. There will be a cost for the container, depending on what is chosen: cardboard coffin, simple coffin, urn, or something more elaborate.

Lastly, home funerals are an option people have started using again. With the advent of the funeral industry in the mid-1800s, funerals moved out of the home and into parlors or mortuaries. Funerals were held in some homes up until the 1930s and '40s. A home funeral allows the family/friends to take on the responsibilities usually handled by the funeral director, and keeps the deceased in the home until disposition. The family would complete the necessary paperwork—death certificate and permit for disposition of remains, and, if applicable, veteran's paperwork. The family can build or buy a casket or purchase a cardboard coffin, depending on the final place of disposition. They would transport the body to the burial site or crematorium, making arrangements for necessary services. If you want a home funeral, I suggest you look into your state's rules and regulations. See Lisa Carlson's book, *Caring for the Dead,* or contact Final Passages or Funeral Consumer's Alliance (contact information is in the resource section at the back of this book). You may need to educate and inform the people who will be involved, including clergy, doctors, family members, and friends, about home funerals. For many it's a new concept.

When I worked with Home Funeral Options, I got a call from a woman with kidney failure. She had already stopped going to dialysis and wanted to plan her death. I met with her and discussed how she wanted to die, where she wanted to be in the house, and how she wanted her sons to be involved. Her sons had never heard of a home funeral and were hesitant about legal issues. I put them in touch with the local public health department, and they were assured that it was legal. At one of our meetings we sat and ate chocolate while we discussed what she wanted to wear and how she wanted her makeup to look. There was laughter and tears. This woman held a party for her friends and talked about her life, the richness of her relationships, her family, and her death. Everyone was moved by the experience.

PLANNING

When someone dies, many things happen, whether the death takes place in the home, hospital, or elsewhere. Emotions are strong. Decisions need to be made. People need to be contacted. Unless well planned, it's usually not a slow, quiet time. Rather, friends and family are being contacted, paperwork is being searched for and reviewed, arrangements are being taken care of, and people are worrying about what to do next.

Making funeral arrangements is one of these activities. If you plan ahead, it can be smoother for those involved. I suggest you plan ahead and fill in this section of this book when you're not in crisis. Having these plans and decisions made and written down well ahead of time allows for a calm setting, and allows loved ones to be in their grief and with each other, rather than discussing or arguing about details.

My intention in writing this section is to inform and educate you about your choices, alert you to some of the risks, and impress upon you the need to be clear and specific about your wishes. I've worked through this process with many families, and the clearer you make it now, the smoother it will be for your loved ones later. I can't stress this enough. It is said that after a home and automobile, a funeral is the largest lifetime expenditure. Take the time to research options and choose what will suit you best.

People have had varied experiences with funeral homes. Some felt completely taken care of and served. Some funeral directors have honored the wishes of the deceased and their surviving family members and friends. Preplanning and payment worked out well. Others have felt taken advantage of and not listened to. There has been confusion, sadness, and anger about how the family was treated. People have said they paid too much and couldn't afford it; others said that they didn't want all the services they bought, but weren't given choices; still others were told that certain practices, such as embalming, were mandatory, though they are not, except in certain circumstances. If you can be definite about your wishes and communicate them clearly to your loved ones or those carrying out your instructions, it will be one of the best gifts you leave. I suggest you contact several funeral homes and ask to pick up their General Price List. Compare services and costs. Then fill in the forms at the end of this section or make a list of your wishes and give copies to family and friends, and the funeral director, if appropriate.

PREPAY

Over the past thirty years, there has been an increase in the number of people who have prepaid their funeral arrangements with a funeral home. For some families this has worked out fine. The intention of pre-paying a funeral is to give you a choice in the type of funeral service you want and give you an opportunity to compare prices. People prepay for various reasons: personal responsibility—"I want to make sure everything is all taken care of and not leave behind any loose ends"; terminal illness—"I don't have long to live and I want to relieve the anxiety of my loved ones at the time of death." People also prepay to lock in a price. Make sure the contract confirms this. Sometimes the family wants the arrangements made while the loved one is still alive because there is emotional stress in filling out the paperwork and making the arrangements. Answers are needed to questions on the death certificate, such as number of years in their occupation, father's and mother's places of birth, and how long they have lived in their community. You can contact the public health department for a copy of a death certificate so you can see what information they require. Also, if the family is making the arrangements while the person is still alive, rather than under stress from his or her recent death, they're not as vulnerable and can find the best prices. If a person dies, this comparison and thought usually can't be done because there is a time factor to be considered. Another reason people prepay is because they want to pay over time to avoid having to pay a lump sum later, or having the family come up with the money.

You can enjoy this same satisfaction by planning ahead and giving this information to those who need to know. You can save your heirs the decision making that takes place at a difficult time and, in some families, avoid conflict between family members who have different ideas, values, or religious beliefs. Letting your family know what you want is critical to having this period go well.

"Without clearly explaining to the survivors exactly what has and has not been paid for, and what to expect, folks are inadvertently—and ironically—guaranteeing heartache and confusion at the time of death," says Joshua Slocum, director of the Funeral Consumers Alliance.

If you want to plan and prepay, below are some options I recommend.

Some people choose to put money in the bank. In some states this is a requirement before entering a nursing home. Here are two options that allow you to put aside money in a financial institution to pay your death expenses. You'll still need to specify exactly what your wishes are, which you can do by completing the pages that follow. Prepaying is important, but explaining your wishes is even more important.

Often known as an irrevocable burial trust, this is money you deposit that can only be used for funeral expenses. The money is put in either a certificate of deposit (CD) or a savings account. The accounts have no penalty when closed at time of death. Interest is earned. Some banks allow you to withdraw interest. Check with your bank on how their program works. The account is taxed. Ask the bank and an attorney about Rights of Survivorship, which means that the account will not go into probate at the time of death. Some banks have a maximum limit of how much can be put into the account. Additionally, if someone has to do a "spend down" to qualify for Medicaid or Medi-Cal, a burial account is a legal way to protect that money. Contact your state's Medicaid/Medi-Cal office for specific limitations. Upon presentation of a certified death certificate, the bank will release the money to the named beneficiary (person who will handle your death arrangements) or to the mortuary of choice. Make sure the named beneficiary knows where the bank paperwork is, what your wishes are and understands the terms for using the money. Check with your tax accountant about the tax ramifications of such an account.

A friend asked me to help her set up an irrevocable burial trust account at our local bank. She wanted her body donated to a medical school and had already contacted the school. We completed the paperwork at the bank, making the local funeral director and me the trustees. She went into a nursing home later and spent down her money. When she died, both the funeral director and I needed to sign paperwork at the bank to release the money. My friend's wishes were honored and her body was a gift to science. This money was protected from probate and used as she wished.

Another option is a Totten Trust. With such a trust, you control the account and can withdraw from it at any time. Money is deposited into a certificate of deposit or money-market account, payable to the beneficiary of your choice, who can be a family member or friend. This account earns interest and is taxed. The funds are immediately available at the time of death without going through probate. This account does not specify that the money be used for a funeral, so choose carefully the beneficiary who'll carry out your funeral wishes. Again, talk to your bank about this option. Consult a tax accountant for tax ramifications.

Making arrangements through a funeral home is another option. A prepaid funeral arrangement is a contract between a mortuary and an individual. This can be in the form of funeral insurance or a contract with a mortuary. Consult with the funeral director and see what they have to offer. When the insurance or contract is used, the signer is dead. There have been problems regarding prepaid funerals. Be aware of what you're signing and what the terms and conditions are. A friend of mine who is a funeral director suggested the following when working with a funeral home, to ensure that you have a valid contract:

1. Ask a witness to accompany you when completing the paperwork with the funeral director.

2. Make sure you are signing a "Guaranteed Funeral Contract."

3. Keep copies of all paperwork and inform your family—especially those who'll take care of your funeral arrangements—of your actions and the location of the paperwork.

4. Ask for a letter on mortuary stationary stating exactly what you paid for, guaranteeing the price and stating there will be no additional fees for the services you paid for. Also, include in the letter the location of where the money is held, and a clause stating that you can transfer the money to another mortuary if necessary.

5. Have the funeral director sign and date the letter.

An elder client of mine decided she wanted to make funeral arrangements for her ill husband prior to his death, knowing that it would be difficult for her later. I called a local, family-owned mortuary, spoke with the funeral director, whom I had worked with before, and we visited her home. I assisted my client in buying funeral insurance, choosing a beautiful casket and a direct burial with no service. She bought exactly what her husband wanted. When her husband died, she waited a few hours before calling the mortuary. The funeral director removed the body, contacted the cemetery, made arrangements with the veterans' office for an honor guard and scheduled the graveside ceremony. This all cost about $1,800. My client was able to spend the time after her husband's death with her family, confident that everything would be taken care of. Issues such as making sure the money is safely held, being able to transfer the policy if you move, being talked into buying more than you want, not getting what you paid for, etc. are decreased if you know the funeral director or know someone who has worked with them.

If your intention is to give your family peace of mind, sensible planning is the best answer. Prepayment may not be necessary and may be risky. AARP takes this position: "AARP advises consumers to pre-plan but not to prepay, largely because pre-need contracts can leave so many important questions unanswered." From the AARP web page, www.aarp.org/bulletin/consumer, November 2002. Pre-need means setting up and paying for funeral arrangements prior to death, usually with a funeral home, or buying funeral insurance.

Pre-plan

Another option is to pre-plan with a funeral home but not pay until after the person dies. Some funeral homes may not want to do this unless death is imminent. Kathy's grandmother was living with her for the previous five years. When the time got close, she and her grandmother talked about final arrangements and Kathy called the local funeral home to plan granny's funeral according to her wishes. When granny died, Kathy contacted the funeral home, which took care of all the arrangements and made the process very easy. Kathy was able to spend that time with family and friends instead of making difficult decisions at the funeral home. Kathy paid for the funeral afterward, but the arrangements were all made ahead of time. Contact your local funeral home about this possibility.

Be a Savvy Consumer

The funeral trade is a multibillion-dollar industry. Everyone who will purchase services needs to be aware of their rights and the funeral home's obligations and rules. The Funeral Consumers Alliance is a national nonprofit organization dedicated to protecting a consumer's right to choose a meaningful, dignified, affordable funeral (see resources for contact information). The FCA offers some suggestions when communicating with a funeral home or mortuary:

1. Ask for their General Price List (GPL). This is one of the most important tools you have for controlling and understanding funeral costs. It lists all the goods and services the funeral home offers, along with the price of each. The GPL allows you to select those items you want and gives you the price for each.

   The Federal Trade Commission set up the Funeral Rule in 1984. It requires funeral directors give customers a copy of the GPL to keep. The GPL must list the prices of specific items—if they are services of the funeral home. These include: the price of a direct cremation and direct burial; cost of basic services of the funeral director and staff, including overhead; cost to prepare the body; cost of embalming; cost of transporting the body; and the cost to use the facility for the viewing, funeral ceremony, or memorial ceremony. The GPL must also include the cost of the funeral vehicle, the range of casket prices and outer burial containers, transportation fees, etc. Previously, the prices were shrouded in secrecy and bundled together into the price of each casket, with no opportunity to buy only some of the services. As a result of FTC response to consumer pressure, this was disallowed, and consumers may now select only the goods and services they desire.

2. Before making any decisions about a funeral, discuss the GPL with family members. It is a good idea to ask the funeral director to leave the room so you can talk in private. If possible, take the GPL home and discuss it. Consider contacting other funeral homes to compare costs and services.

3. Look in the GPL for the itemized list of services. Funeral homes can offer packages of services at a discount over the itemized cost of each service. This is only a bargain if you would have chosen those services anyway. The packages usually appear at the beginning of the GPL, and can confuse you into thinking that that's all there is. Regardless of whether you pre-plan or have to make an urgent decision, reviewing the GPL is important in making wise choices.

Here are the simplest options: A direct cremation or immediate burial. Services of the funeral home include picking up the body, the basic services fee, filing the death certificate and disposition permit and transportation to the crematory or cemetery. If you want more elaborate services—memorial service at the funeral home, embalming, viewing of the body, use of funeral vehicles—there will be a basic fee plus additional fees for each desired service. The basic fee is the only fee on the price list that the customer cannot avoid paying, no matter what option you choose. Originally, this fee was intended to cover services common to most arrangements: filing the paperwork, coordinating plans with the cemetery and crematory, and contacting Social Security, the Department of Veterans Affairs, and insurance companies. You can shop around and see what different funeral homes offer.

The General Price List must also list a price range of available caskets and vaults. Before showing the merchandise, the funeral director must show you a fully itemized list of available caskets and vaults. If the least expensive caskets are not on display, ask to see them. There may be a variety of colors or types available that are not shown; ask what else is available. A family can provide a casket and not be charged by the funeral home. See Funeral Consumer's Alliance's webpage. There are businesses that sell coffins directly to family members, or you can make your own. Search the Internet for options. When doing a home funeral, the casket often plays a role in the rituals the family creates. Caskets can be cardboard or simple wood, or elaborate. This is one place where knowing what's available can make a difference in price and sentiment.

"It really pays to know what choices are available before death. General ignorance of the workings of the death and burial industries, and ignorance of our options, causes us to be complicit in keeping funeral prices high because we don't exercise savvy in the purchase." So says Joshua Slocum, executive director of Funeral Consumer's Alliance, on the website of P.O.V.—A Family Undertaking (see resource list for contact information).

There are excellent resources available that inform consumers of their rights and empower us regarding end-of-life care. Contact the Funeral Consumers Alliance, Department of Veterans Affairs, AARP, the Federal Trade Commission, et al, for information, and see the resources listed in the back of this book.

Throughout this section I have suggested you speak to your loved ones about your thoughts and plan what you want done. I realize this may be challenging. I encourage you to be persistent in your efforts to inform and educate them on your behalf and theirs; and fill in this section so you have it down on paper. Make copies and give them to those who'll be carrying out your wishes.

These are my instructions for (name person responsible): _____

I want to:

- ❑ *be buried*

- ❑ *be cremated*

- ❑ *be entombed in a mausoleum, crypt, vault (circle one)*

- ❑ *donate my organs (complete section below)*

- ❑ *bequeath my body to a medical school (see section below)*

- ❑ *have my "agent," named on my Advance Directive / Durable Power of Attorney for Health Care / Five Wishes, decide*

- ❑ *have my next of kin decide*

- ❑ *other:* _____

I have prepaid the funeral expenses or have set aside $ _____

- ❑ *with a mortuary (name):* _____

- ❑ *with a funeral-insurance company (name):* _____

- ❑ *with a bank — Irrevocable Trust Account (name):* _____

- ❑ *with a cemetery / memorial park (name):* _____

- ❑ *other:* _____

I have already paid for the following:

- ❑ *casket*

- ❑ *funeral arrangements*

- ❑ *cemetery plot, crypt, mausoleum, vault (circle one)*

- ❑ *cremation*

- ❑ *home funeral*

- ❑ *other:* _____

Location of Records for Prepaid Funeral: _____

If you prefer not to prepay, state your wishes on the expense of the arrangements:

❑ under $1000   ❑ $1000–$3000   ❑ $3000–$5000

❑ $5000–$8000   ❑ $8000–$10,000   ❑ over $10,000

❑ other: ....

Regarding the service, I want *(mark the appropriate boxes)*:

❑ *a service with body present*

❑ *a service with body absent*

❑ *an open casket*

❑ *a closed casket*

❑ *a viewing with family only*

❑ *a memorial with remains present*

❑ *a memorial with remains absent*

❑ *a graveside service*

❑ *a military service*

❑ *no service*

❑ *to have my next of kin decide*

❑ *to have my "agent," named on my Advance Directive / Durable Power of Attorney for Health Care / Five Wishes, decide*

❑ *other:* ....

I want:

❑ *a casket. Type:* ....

❑ *a plain pine or wooden casket*

❑ *a cardboard casket*

❑ *other:* ....

Veterans

Veterans are eligible for a flag, a military marker, and a plot in a military cemetery. For more information, ask the funeral director. Contact your local VA regional office. If you're unable to locate your records, contact the National Personnel Records Center (see resources section at the back of this book).

Embalming

Embalming is not required within the first 24 hours in any state in the United States. Some states require embalming after 24, 48, or 72 hours, but refrigeration is usually an accepted option. Check *Caring for the Dead,* by Lisa Carlson. This book has state-by-state regulations and contact information for state agencies that can answer your questions. If the body is being shipped across state lines, then embalming is required in Alabama, Alaska, and New Jersey (2005). If a common carrier is used to ship, Kansas, Minnesota, and Idaho require embalming if the body is shipped from those states. There is no federal regulation requiring that a body be embalmed if shipped on a common carrier. Contact your local public health department for updated regulations. Delta Airlines will transport a body that is not embalmed (see resources for contact information).

❑ *I want to be embalmed.*

❑ *I do not want to be embalmed.*

❑ *I want my next of kin to decide.*

If I am cremated, I want my ashes:

❑ *placed in a simple container*

❑ *placed in a more expensive container*

❑ *scattered at the cemetery*

❑ *scattered at sea* ❑ *by airplane* ❑ *by boat*

❑ *kept in the home*

❑ *buried at this location:* _____

❑ *other:* _____

HOME FUNERAL

If I have a home- or family-directed funeral, I want my coordinator / director to be:*

_____

❑ *I want to lie in honor for _____ days.*

❑ *I want to lie on a bed*   ❑ *on a draped table*   ❑ *in a disposition container (casket)*

❑ *In which part of the house?* _____

❑ *I want the room I am lying in to have music, flowers, candles, or mementos, etc. Be specific.*

_____

_____

❑ *I want my cardboard or wood casket decorated by friends and family.*

MARKER

Do you want a marker for the grave site?   *YES   NO*

❑ *monument*

❑ *headstone*

❑ *flat marker*

❑ *other:* _____

What words do you want on the marker?

_____

_____

_____

* See "Final Passages and Transformations" in resource section for instruction on how to do a home funeral.

Organ Donation

Laws regarding organ donation vary from state to state. The Coalition on Donation web page provides a state-by-state guide to donation (see resource section for contact information).

My organ-donor card is located: _____

_____

I want:

❑ *All of my body donated*

❑ *Specific parts:* _____

❑ *I want my remains to be returned to my family for scattering*

❑ *I want the hospital to dispose of my ashes*

❑ *Other:* _____

Bequest to a Medical School

A bequest to a medical school must be made ahead of time. See the Florida Anatomical Board or National Anatomical Services for a listing of the schools nearest to you.

Arrangements are made with: _____

Address: _____

_____

Phone: _____   *Fax:* _____

I want:

❑ *my remains to be returned to my family for scattering.*

  Where? _____

❑ *the medical school to dispose of my ashes.*

OBITUARY/DEATH NOTICE

Depending on where you live and who you are, there are choices to make regarding a public notice about your death. There are two types of announcements: obituaries and death notices. A death notice is a paid announcement, with family gathering the relevant information and giving it to the mortuary, which submits it to the newspaper. An obituary is a story written by the newspaper staff as a news item, usually at no cost. In small communities, local newspapers often publish obituaries provided by the family at no cost. Contact your local newspaper to ask about their procedure.

If you want an obituary written, whom do you want to write it?

What do you want written in the obituary (date and place of birth, names of survivors, education and employment record, military service, achievements, offices held, recipient of donations in lieu of flowers, time and place of funeral or memorial service)?

If you choose to write your own, include a copy here and let responsible persons know about it:

Which newspaper(s) do you want the obituary to appear in?

Do you want notes sent to clients, colleagues? YES NO

If yes, list who should receive notes:

FUNERAL SERVICE/MEMORIAL CELEBRATION

A funeral service is usually done at the funeral home or church, with the body present. A memorial celebration/service is usually done after the disposition of the body.

Do you want a funeral service? YES NO

Do you want a memorial celebration? YES NO

If yes, what do you envision and where do you want it to be held?

What special prayers, sayings, songs, hymns, or music do you want at the service?

Do you want food? YES NO

If yes, describe what you would like:

Whom do you want included in the service or celebration? You could use the contact sheet in this book (next page), mark names in your address book, or list the names here.

If you prefer your address book to be used, where do you keep it?

CONTACT LISTS

PEOPLE TO CONTACT BY PHONE AT TIME OF DEATH
(use an asterisk * to mark the names of relatives)

Name:

Phone Number:

Name:

Phone Number:

Name:

Phone Number:

Name:

Phone Number:

Name:

Phone Number:

Name:

Phone Number:

Name:

Phone Number:

Name:

Phone Number:

Name:

Phone Number:

Name:

Phone Number:

Name:

Phone Number:

People to Contact by Mail, Fax, or E-mail at Time of Death

Name:

Address:

Fax: *E-mail Address:*

Name:

Address:

Fax: *E-mail Address:*

Name:

Address:

Fax: *E-mail Address:*

Name:

Address:

Fax: *E-mail Address:*

Name:

Address:

Fax: *E-mail Address:*

Name:

Address:

Fax: *E-mail Address:*

Name:

Address:

Fax: *E-mail Address:*

Name:

Address:

Fax: *E-mail Address:*

Name:

Address:

Fax: *E-mail Address:*

Name:

Address:

Fax: *E-mail Address:*

Name:

Address:

Fax: *E-mail Address:*

Document Location / Checklist

Write the locations of all of the following; be as specific as you can:

Social Security cards

Passport

Citizenship Papers

Will (Original / Copies)

Trust (Original / Copies)

Advanced Health Care Directive / Five Wishes

DNR (Do Not Resuscitate) Order

Donor Card

Birth Certificates

Marriage Certificates

Domestic Partner Registration Form

Prenuptial Agreement

Child / Spousal Support Agreement

Divorce Papers

Adoption Papers

Death Certificates

Medical Records

Insurance Records

Education Records, Diplomas, Transcripts

Photos / Video of Insured Items

Current and Unpaid Bills

Military Records

Address Book

Promissory Notes

Bank Records

Checkbook

Savings Passbook

Canceled Checks

Pink Slip / Vehicle Registration

Tax Records

Safe-deposit Key(s)

Credit Card Records

Investment Records

Real Estate Records

Appraisals

Income Records

Loan Agreements

Business Records

End-of-life Instructions

Prepaid Cemetery Contract

Prepaid Funeral Contract

Warranties / Instructions

Post Office Box Keys

Citizenship Papers / Green Card

Home Inventory

Household Safe

Work-related Papers

Transferable Frequent-flyer Miles

Other:

Resources

A Family Undertaking, a film by Elizabeth Westrate, explores the growing home funeral movement (see webpage **www.pbs.org/pov/pov2004/afamilyundertaking/index.html**). Their website also features a chronology of dying in America, an "ask the experts" panel, and a discussion guide.

American Anatomical Transport will tell you where the closest medical institution is located for a full-body donation. Phone 800-727-0700.

American Veterans Institute. Among other services, the American Veterans Institute supports programs spotlighting the availability of VA benefits. **www.americanveteransinstitute.org**

Better Business Bureau's *Wise Giving* can assist you in making informed giving decisions. The guide evaluates national charities that have been the subject of inquiries received by the BBB. These evaluations include nonprofit fundraising practices, programs, finances, and governance. They evaluate these issues against the *BBB Standards for Charity Accountability.* You can order a guide by contacting the BBB Wise Giving Guide. Their address is 4200 Wilson Blvd., Suite 800, Arlington, VA 22203; phone 703-276-0100, e-mail charities@cbbb.bbb.org; website www.give.org.

Caring for the Dead: Your Final Act of Love, by Lisa Carlson, Upper Access, Inc., 1998. This book is a complete guide to making funeral arrangements with or without a funeral director, and lists the rules of all fifty states. Lisa is a former director of FCA.

Coalition on Donation is a nonprofit alliance of national organizations and local coalitions across the United States that have joined forces to educate the public about organ, eye, and tissue donation. Their website, www.donatelife.net, allows you to choose a state and find out how you can become a donor. Contact them at 804-782-4920 or e-mail coalition@donatelife.net.

Delta Airlines has a program called Delta Care that transports coffins nationally and internationally. Dry ice or gel packs can be used instead of embalming. Phone Delta at 800-352-2737. Check with your public health department and the airlines for specific rules and regulations.

Department of Veterans Affairs should be contacted if your loved one served in the military. You may be eligible for benefits. Call 800-827-1000 or visit www.va.gov.

Federal Trade Commission offers informative, concise, easy-to-read information about the funeral industry in their guide, *Funerals: A Consumer Guide.* They discuss preneed, planning, and prepaying on a funeral, and explain the different kinds of funerals, the Funeral Rule, and choosing a funeral provider. The website explains the various costs and lists services and products available. They also provide a worksheet to track the costs when you call various funeral homes, a glossary of terms and a resource list. Call them at 800-501-4550. The website is www.ftc.gov/bcp/conline/pubs/services/funeral.htm.

Five Wishes is the first living will that talks about your personal, emotional, and spiritual needs as well as your medical wishes. In some states it can replace the Advance Directive for Health Care/Durable Power of Attorney for Health Care. For copies, call 888-594-7437, write to Aging with Dignity, PO Box 1661, Tallahassee, FL 32302-1661, or visit www.agingwithdignity.org.

Florida Anatomical Board lists all the body-donation programs by state on their website, www.med.ufl.edu. Call them at 800-628-2594, or e-mail anatbd@dean.med.ufl.edu.

Final Passages is a Northern California nonprofit program dedicated to a natural approach of home and family-directed funerals. Jerri Grace Lyons teaches courses in how to do family directed funerals throughout the United States. She has assisted with hundreds of home funerals over the past ten years. Final Passages has publications that direct you in how to do your own home funeral. They can be reached at PO Box 1721, Sebastopol, CA 95473; phone 707-824-0268; e-mail info@final-passages.org; website: www.finalpassages.org.

Funeral Consumers Alliance is the umbrella organization for funeral and memorial societies in the U.S. They provide educational materials on funeral choices, monitor the funeral industry, advocate on a national level, provide leadership for local memorial and funeral societies, and refer individuals to appropriate societies and agencies supplying local services. Societies are available to help you understand you options, inform you of fair pricing, and let you know of reputable providers. For help in locating a society near you, contact FCA at 800-765-0107 or visit www.funerals.org. Local societies, which are usually run by volunteers, do price surveys of local mortuaries, crematoria, and cemeteries. For society members, they may negotiate prices with local funeral homes. FCA's webpage has information on pre-planning/prearranging funerals, funeral home ethics, caskets and urns, and veterans' funeral and burial benefits. FCA has information on the reasons people spend too much for a funeral, the pitfalls of paying for a funeral ahead of time, the facts about embalming, and many other important issues. Visit their website.

Insurance Information Institute is an organization whose mission is to improve the public's understanding of insurance. It is a primary source of information, analysis and referrals concerning insurance. III publishes pamphlets and books. Call 212-346-

5500, write them at 110 Williams St., New York, NY 10038, or visit www.iii.org.

Medical alarm companies help seniors and those with chronic medical conditions to live independently. Many programs provide a personal help button and a base unit that connects to an alarm company responder who is trained to evaluate your situation. Contact your hospital to find a company that serves your area, or go online and search "medical alarm companies." Assistance is available through state programs to help pay for this service—contact your hospital or home health program.

National Anatomical Service gives listings of medical schools that accept body donations. Call 800-727-0700.

National Association of Professional Organizers (NAPO) is a not-for-profit professional association formed in 1985. Dedicated to sharing information about the growing organizing industry, its trends, and its concerns, NAPO works to set and define quality standards for the organizing profession. NAPO members include organizing consultants, speakers, trainers, authors, and manufacturers of organizing products. Their website allows you to find an organizer in your area: www.napo.net.

National Personnel Records Center is the repository of millions of military records including medical, personnel, and health. You can order a copy of a veteran's military record by mail using Standard Form 180. You can download this form from the web or call for a copy. National Personnel Records Center, 9700 Page Blvd., St. Louis, MO 63132-5100, Tel: 314-801-0800, webpage: www.vetrecs.archives.gov.

Nolo Press publishes self-help legal products in book, software, and e-book form that cover topics such as wills and estate planning, landlords and tenants, debt and bankruptcy, real estate, probate, and living trusts. They can be reached at 800-728-3555, on the Web at www.nolo.com, or at 950 Parker Street, Berkeley, CA 94701-2524.

Sidekick, Your home reference book is a fill-in-the-blank reference book that enables you to store information about every aspect of your home, from warranty information, room sizes, paint colors, appliance models, serial numbers, and window measurements, to room diagrams. It includes places to keep samples: paint chips, fabric swatches, carpet pieces, and receipts—the uses are limitless. See their webpage, www.thesidekick.net, or call 866-203-8034.

Transformations is a nonprofit organization that provides meaningful information and guidance for compassionate living and dying. They have three programs: Home Care Guides—a caregiver training program; Being with Dying—family consultations and a workshop; and Home Funeral Options—alternatives to traditional funeral practices. Contact them at their website: www.transformationsincare.org.

ABOUT THE AUTHOR

 MAGGIE WATSON, the second of ten children, was born near Philadelphia, Pennsylvania. Always active in her community, she created a Social Awareness Committee at East Stroudsburg University, and later became a Peace Corps volunteer in West Africa. A professional organizer for more than fifteen years, she operates her own business, called Simple Systems. In addition, she organizes for the elderly, allowing them to continue living independently in their homes. She has led county-wide workshops on the importance of completing the document called "The Five Wishes," and is especially interested in empowering people to make informed decisions. Ms. Watson lives in northern California with her husband, Bruce, and son Julian.

ORDER FORM

A GRACEFUL FAREWELL: *Putting Your Affairs in Order*

Please photocopy this form to order workbooks to share with family and friends.

Number of books ordered @ $19.95 _____   Subtotal: $_____

Sales Tax 7.75% (California residents only) $_____

Shipping and handling: $4 Media Mail or $7.00 UPS or Priority Mail
Please add $1 for each additional book. $_____

Total: $_____

SHIP TO:

Name: _____

Address: _____

City: _____ State: _____ Zip: _____

CREDIT CARD TYPE: ❏ MasterCard   ❏ VISA   ❏ Discover   ❏ AmEx

Credit Card No. _____

Expiration: _____

Your name as it appears on your credit card: _____

Authorized cardholder signature: _____

Billing Address: _____

City: _____ State: _____ Zip: _____

Daytime Telephone: _____

GIFT CARD INFORMATION

From: _____

To: _____

Address: _____

City: _____ State: _____ Zip: _____

Mail your order and check to:

Cypress House · 155 Cypress Street · Fort Bragg, CA 95437
Call **800-773-7782**, or fax your credit card order to **707-964-7531**.
Order online: **www.cypresshouse.com**